To my family, Tom and the little peach, whoever you are.
You all helped shape this book. Thank you.

BIG PICTURE PRESS

This edition published in the UK in 2023 by Big Picture Press.
First published in the UK in 2022 by Big Picture Press
an imprint of Bonnier Books UK
4th Floor, Victoria House
Bloomsbury Square, London WC1B 4DA
Owned by Bonnier Books
Sveavägen 56, Stockholm, Sweden
www.bonnierbooks.co.uk

1 3 5 7 9 10 8 6 4 2

ISBN 978-1-80078-225-9

This book was typeset in Cabrito Didone
The illustrations were created with watercolour,
pencil and ink and finished digitally

Written by Lily Murray
Edited by Isobel Boston and Carly Blake
Designed by Olivia Cook
Production by Che Creasey

Printed in China

MIX
Paper | Supporting
responsible forestry
FSC® C020056

Sarah Maycock

Love
is ...

BPP

Love is

LOUD,

like a peacock proudly flashing
its iridescent eyes for all to see.

But sometimes love sings a quieter song,
soft as the evening chorus,
but no less strong.

Love is

PLAyfUL,

like meerkats
rolling in the dust.

But love can be serious too . . .
looking out for each other,
when times are tough.

Love is

DARING,

like a bear cub exploring
the world for the first time.

But love is also comforting,
offering a safe embrace to remind
us that tomorrow is a new day.

Love is
POWERFUL,
like the strength and passion
of tigers in the wild.

But love is also gentle,
and full of tender moments.

Love is

BEAUTIFUL,

like the sanctuary
a bowerbird builds for its mate –
adorned with treasures.

But love's beauty comes
in many different forms . . .

. . . a simple song,

a colourful dance,

a loving face.

Love is

ENDURING,

spanning generations.

But even if love is fleeting,
it lives on in memories, smiles and stories.

Love is

BOLD,

like an orangutan
climbing high to reach
the ripest fruit.

But love can also be soft and caring,
considering the needs of others.

Love is

BEING TOGETHER,

like whales swimming side by side,

forging a powerful bond.

But everyone needs time by themselves,
to think, explore and be free . . .

. . . and that too, is love.

Love is

FAST

and fleet-footed,

like wild hares leaping
        through long grass.

But love that takes its time . . .

. . . is no less rewarding.

Love is a

POWERFUL THING,

For with love . . .

We can do

ANYTHING.